HOME.
GIRL.
HOOD.

Ebony Stewart

HOME.
GIRL.
HOOD.

Edited by: Ariana Brown & Michael Whalen
Interior Art by: Alice Chipkin & Ammar Nsoroma
Interior design by: Allison Truj

BUTTON PUBLISHING INC.
MINNEAPOLIS
2022

© 2022 by Ebony Stewart

◆

butt⬤n p⬤etry

Published by Button Poetry / Exploding Pinecone Press
Minneapolis, MN 55403 | http://www.buttonpoetry.com

◆

All Rights Reserved
Manufactured in the United States of America
Cover art & design: Madison Escoffrey & Martin Thomas
ISBN 978-1-63834-007-2

2025 2024 2023 2022 2021   1 2 3 4 5

to the hearts that hear me
beating the pain away
sis with the twist out a closed fist
a walk like we mean-it
the girls who be human mostly womxn &
the boys who we don't have to beg to love us

Contents

Cultural Appropriation vs. Appreciation	3
Hairtage	4
Lilith	6
Psst… Ayo B*tch! Lemme Holla At Chu	9
How To Write A Poem About Sexual Assault	11
An Ode To My Pussy	13
Eve	15
Rooftop Rendezvous	18
How To Properly Flirt With Someone You're Attracted To	19
Contacts: Names I Changed Your Name To	21
Electrolytes	22
(still waiting…)	24
Today Must Be	25
Interlude	28
Happy Father's Day	31
On The Way Back To Myself	36
I Am	38
What We Become	40
I got some friends Black when it's convenient	43
Re-Conditioning	45
Slapboxing	47
Compassion Fatigue	49
Perhaps we should go back	51
Family Tree	53
Fear	55
I Love Mondays	57
Happy Mother's Day	60
I'm So Tired…	62

Preface

I started writing poetry when I was around eight or nine years old. It should be noted I got into writing poetry by way of journaling in therapy after my parents very abusive relationship came to an end. Somewhere in my childhood I just stopped talking, so my mother took me to see a therapist. Naturally (and still) I was very hesitant to anyone new in my life, especially if they asked questions I perceived as none of their business. The therapist handed me a composition journal and told me to write as much as I wanted, and when I was ready, I could let her read it. I should say, I learned early on not to be so eager to befriend or trust white people, so it took a long while for me to share. When I finally did, the therapist read my journal, prescribed me Xanax, and said I was suffering from depression. I was nine (maybe ten). Growing up in Baytown, TX (more hood than suburb right outside of Houston, TX.), in a single parent household, there was all kinds of trauma I was experiencing without knowing it. But like many educators and health providers who can't relate or recognize post-traumatic stress disorder in Black children, the need for care and concern was dismissed. The therapist did, however, introduce me to a coping technique that would catapult a new form of expressing the uninterrupted freedom to think, hurt, and heal no matter how big or small, elaborate or precise, beautiful or ugly the truth was. I am someone who knows poetry as a great tool for looking in & building out.

In undergrad, I learned the combination of me being Black, woman, and a writer also made me a threat. I majored in English and Communication Studies. I became very aware of the placement of words, how they were used to criticize and work against me; how careful I had to be in communicating and advocating for myself; tone, inflection, meaning, reason -- Black kids (especially Black girls) always have to keep their creativity in check. In college, every professor, except two, told me I was a poor writer and never had clear and consecutive thoughts. One was adamant my writing was mediocre at best and I wouldn't be a successful writer.

The translation of his racial bias stemmed from the difference in which we were individually allowed to experience the world based on race, social and economic class, age, and gender. I was always writing from what I experience, and he was always reading from an agency of privilege.

That criticism wrecked me. I'm not sure I've ever really gotten over it. I still have a hard time believing that my writing makes sense or is any good. *Home.Girl.Hood.* Home Girl. Home = Hood. Girlhood. Hood Girl. is for every hood, every block, every Black girl wonder that ever lived and didn't always use proper grammar, didn't go to college, didn't fit into academic spaces, or that academia doesn't make space for. *Home.Girl.Hood.* is for every dark skin Black girl, for Black girls, for girls that take up space, transcends, and name they don't know, yet. *Home.Girl.Hood.* is a multifaceted work that explores queerness, misogynoir, and womanhood. More than anything, *Home.Girl.Hood.* is an offering to myself, I hope you can relate to what's inside, but it's quite possible, this body of work might not be for you–and that's okay.

Welcome, to *Home.Girl.Hood.*

HOME.
GIRL.
HOOD.

Cultural Appropriation vs. Appreciation
a pop quiz

A white girl describes her matted and curly mess, kinky. Say it be 'fro/but she ain't never had to make a fist in her life. Ask me to explain cultural appropriation but really she asking for permission. Say she ain't like the others. Ask me to call her ally and still let all her privilege stand in front of me. Or at least continue to save face when she get to be wounded. 'Cause white people get to be sad and savior. Want me to forget serial killer white men kill her but literally everyone is trying to kill me. Want me to stop calling her Becky. Ask me to learn her real name or at least be sensitive to all the actual Beckys out there. Don't want me to say nothing when she mishandles me, when she call me "boo" say, "yaaaas," or dance to Beyonce's Formation like it was made for her because, we're womyn, right? How she get to say, "bye Felicia" and leave the party a stolen identity. Knowing she don't know 'nere Felicia or even where that saying came from no way. Ask me if she can try on my struggle. Say she wanna make a fashion statement/ when ere'thing I am and been through, made me this way. And we ain't equal. Not because she say so, but because she ain't never had to be a choir, a chorus, and defeat...and still have to teach ere'body the song, the dance moves, AND not get paid, AND give away my own praise, AND watch her accept an award that probably belongs to me.

Hairitage

"My skin is Black
My arms are long
My hair is woolly
My back is strong
Strong enough to take the pain
Inflicted again and again"
-Nina Simone

Black angels are descending. And my mother's words are divided into quadrants. In a single plait, she interlaces stories, arranges strength, and teaches patterns. Gifts. Hands are no longer hands, they are technique. Transferring information. I am nappy around my edges. Saying, my roots haven't always been free.

My mother says we laid across each other like shackled berets on slave ships. And they killed the natives so she wasn't told how many times we've been called out our name. Said, my grandmother sung strands of gospel anyway, Negro Spirituals in the way she braids. She is beautiful, in the way she braids, weaving…mistakes,to remind me that there will always be a hair out of place and there will never be enough time to fix it, so tread lightly, braid carefully.

She, my mother, uses words like rivers made up of tears. I can still feel the waves of how many times she's wanted to cry but refuses to acknowledge pain as an intricate pleat of beauty. So I ask, "Can I just be a ponytail, mama!?" "Braids take too long… and my head hurts!" She told me, that wasn't her, that was society. Some people are more comfortable with us walking narrow, looking fine. She says, when your hair's a mess they think your life is too. And I shouldn't give them the satisfaction of knowing my business better than me. My mother uses one hand to keep me in place, while the other hand is a rubber band pulled tight like grandma's grip on family. She makes a knot and says, this is a fist, for whenever you are weak you are also strong.

And I wanted to go back. Look back to when I was more than just a color. Light skin. Dark skin. Ebony is always in. My mother calls me pretty. She says all Black girls are, and how could our hair not be the source of what makes us grow? Don't be brittle in your strength or judge character based on length. You have no idea what I did to get here, in this moment.

I am a womxn. And the only difference is the way I hold my head, and even that was inherited. See tomorrow we can start over, but today, we gotta walk like we flawless with a theme song. And so when I'm undone, when I'm naked in the sunlight holding the moon in the palm of my hand, we are linked up. And my mother is still transferring information, through gifts we call hands.

Lilith

                        I'll be Lilith.
First to be done dirty
                                        and erased.
"She who sits young while the earth is old."[1]
                    womxn with snakes growing from her head.
                        womxn who art dangerous,
who uses the word "no" like men do   and means it,
who opens her legs wide and takes up just as much space.
                      Womxn who refused to fake it,
                              because clit,
                            because orgasms,
                            because laughter.

She who will not submit.
She who will not be silent or tolerant,
shame, shield, or sheet.
She who took all her fruit
                and fuck yo garden.
She who jumped.
                         Womxn who went tribal
grew wings & claws
from a tramp stamp.
                         Womxn who beeth cunt
                         and hath more to give.
She who didn't get put out.
She who belongeth to herself.
                                    Wholly.

She who left his straight neck bent,
to the tree of knowledge.
She who was also betrayed
and the one who taketh blame.

---

[1]   *Lady Lilith* & "Eden bower" by Dante Gabriel Rossetti

Lilith.
Womxn who would not hold your wounds
or your sorries.
Womxn without a last name.

She who will not return to her
oppressors.
She who has enough colonizers.
Who gave birth to too many
misogynists
       wanna tell her what to do with her
                                    uterus.
                         Womxn of Pangea.

She who art picked apart,
                                picked last,
         they come for first.
She whose milk doesn't have
an expiration date.
She who washes her own bloody
panties by hand.
She who lives harassment daily.
                       Body of logical fears.

She who doesn't bite her nails
but has other bad habits:
                                  Talks back.
                        Forgot to suck it in,
                          shave her legs,
                          paint her toes.
She who still can't figure out
                   how to make a proper wing
                   with her eyeliner stick.
She who carries weight
            and still be fly.
She who did not ask
for your permission
                             to love a womxn.
She who does not also date
                             womyn because

    she be confused
                      or ain't had it right.
She who made her own
                choices.
          The question is not whether
she can get the D,
              but the answer is,
                    womxn who does not want it
                    or womxn who requires more.
She who is cavalier to
your opinion of her
                choices.
She who is trained in:
        intentionality and hood
        M60 bus and 125th
shotgun and
                            semi-automatic.
        Consider this whole poem anything
            but a warning shot.
                    Womxn of tambourine.
                          NOLA clap.
                              Twerk.
                6 selfies & kept all of em.
She who showed up
one day in heels.
The next day
combat boots.
                    Womxn who art comfortable
                                and
                            okay with
        not being
        consumed.

Psst... Hey Yo B*tch!
Let Me Holla At Chu

A man is yelling something obscene out his car window one night
and I am stupid womxn
walking home alone
now holding my breath—
knowing he thinks me something beautiful and meek or feisty.
See my jawbone clenching and that's probably what's got his dick hard.
The womyn in my family are raising all the men born to us like gods,
but as soon as we turn our backs,
they behave like dogs without leashes or wedding rings.
I hear him lick his lips,
and suddenly, all the men I know are apologizing for what they too
have done to someone's daughter.
I do not give him an eyebrow, a mouth twitch, a hot or cold shoulder—
just the corners of my eyes so he know I see him.
Men are easily annoyed when we pretend not to see them.

I used to think men are used to rejection,
then Mary Spears was killed for saying "no."
So maybe they aren't.
I used to think womyn were used to being hounded,
then Janese Jackson was killed for ignoring Charles McKinney's advances.
So maybe we aren't.
Therefore,
I am mindful of masculinity.
I know to be this way because I call the oldest man in my family
with the most fragile ego,
grandpa.

When he honks his horn
or blows me a kiss

and calls me names I do not own,
I wonder if he's bothering me because he's bored
or
is this the way he catches everything he hunts?
There are plenty of men who do things because they've been hurt
and don't know what to do with their pain.
One of them is my father.
Therefore,
there will always be
men who have solutions
and men who cause problems.
Sometimes, they are one and the same.

When he drives away...
When I'm safe and alive in my own body belonging to me...
Then,
and only then,
can I breathe.

How To Write A Poem About Sexual Assault
*(after Mahogany L. Browne's
How to Write A Poem About Ferguson)*

How to write a poem about sexual assault or rape or thin lines or how to be a womxn and give up everything you have or she didn't ask for it or what makes a womxn a slut or ask a womxn or womyn slut shame womyn or what she got on ain't got nothing to do with how she should be treated or how loud or how many times or what are different ways to say no or stop or I changed my mind or please or or or......... how to ask for help or how to be the victim or how to be victim blamed or how to be catcalled and keep doing/anything/ or how to have legs or a booty or breasts or a pussy or how to have private body parts that don't get touched or how to be a womxn that isn't a person or how to lighten up or how to smile without being interrupted or how to take a joke or how to act like you didn't hear the joke or how to know it was a joke or how to know something wrong was said in the first place or how to cry on the inside or how to keep people out of your insides or how to keep your mouth shut or okay or whatever or how to shoo someone away as your only defense or how to write a poem about being a womxn or how to remind a girl of what to expect when she becomes a womxn or every last womxn in here has a story which means every man in here has a story or I'm sorry or how to apologize to everyone in here with a story or how to love a womxn who has a story or how to love a wom-xn who trusts no one or how to be a womxn who trusts no one or how to match hope with your clothing or how to wipe a body clean or how to talk without bursting or how to give up space or how to be small or big or broken or none of those or how to write a poem about healing or forgiveness or remembering less or pretending it didn't happen or being immune to the fact that it keeps happening or there is no ending to this poem or this poem has no ending or every time a girl is born she's the new ending to this poem or it happens to boys too or sad facts or it shouldn't be a competition or I don't know how to end this poem because this poem has no ending or how to write a poem about ending sexual assault or rape or has it stopped happening, yet...

An Ode To My Pussy

This is an ode to my pussy
'cause somebody don't want me
to celebrate my pussy,
wanna shame my pussy,
wanna own my pussy.
Keep asking who this pussy belong to...

        IT'S MINE, MUTHAFUCKA!
        Always has been, always will be
        MY PUSSY!

It's a wonder my pussy ain't drowned you yet,
'cause I run these seas, all 7 of 'em.
My pussy open her mouth too wide
or get too shook and my pussy'll shake the whole Earth a loose.
This be the power of Pussy!
Could suffocate you if she wanted to,
but look how much of you my pussy keep sparin'.
All praises to God, Allah, my pussy, and menses.
My pussy don't douche!
My pussy got enough saucy self-cleaning functions to clean herself.
So my pussy still smell like,
sound like,
taste like,
and feel like
PUSSY!

My pussy might fuck you once and never wanna fuck you again,
because my pussy get to say who,
my pussy get to say when.
My pussy don't grab back,
because my pussy ain't interested in taking anything that don't
belong to her.

This pussy also has a womb,
has had an abortion and ain't ashamed of it,
'cause this pussy chose herself for herself.
And even if this pussy never has a child or can't have a child,
this pussy still be pussy, be womxn, and worthy as fuck.

This pussy wants you to stop wondering how trans pussy works
or where they go to the bathroom.
This pussy say,
you worried about the wrong things,
and where the fuck you think pussy been going to the bathroom!?

My pussy says,
stop comparing my pussy to fragile things when you really mean
testicles or masculinity or anything else that it's only response to
fear is to shrink or cower or duck out.
My pussy ain't got that option.
'Cause everybody know,
don't shit get done, 'til my pussy show up.
You must not understand the gravitas of my pussy—
the holy magic, durability, and genius that be my pussy.
Chil', my pussy ain't stuttin' you.
Couldn't give a damn or a fuck if you like my pussy,
'cause my pussy gets free by
saying
and
doing
whatever
the
fuck
it
wants!

Eve

> "Womxn does not emerge from man's ribs. Not ever. It is he who emerges from her womb." -Nizar Qabbani

1.
In the beginning,
God told Eve she did not need a man to exist.
It is he who keeps hissing to be born.
It is he who only has a rib to give.
It is your choice.
Your body to stew blood and eat your own fruit with.
You have all the ribs you need, God said.
This will only be balloon acting as bone.
Eve said, let it float.
I'll teach him how to protect my heart.
Then after, man will have purpose.

2.
He asked if he could touch her.
This is back when man knew
womxn as human;
more than an afterthought.
Remembered when womxn was more
than a safe place to rest.
Man, remember to ask, can I touch your holy?
Eve said, yes.
Drowned him in all her grace.
Wrote him an ocean's worth.
He asked if he could put it in her mouth.
She said,
I am still speaking.
He said,
swallow me.

She said,
I am still tasting myself.
He said,
teach me how to give birth.
She said,
you cannot handle the war wombs bring.
I'm made of geography. I know this land.
Hips and thighs.
How sweet it is.

3.
For several months, Eve is a forest fire.
Makes her body a place no one can afford.
Feels like she let someone borrow her
and now they never want to give her back.
There is a quiet riot inside me, Eve said.
Anyone who says womyn are delicate and breakable,
can't remember the ways in which they were born.

4.
She grits her teeth.
Stretching her bones and eyes wide.
Man can only offer breathing.
He is still afloat.
The room smells like shit and burning sky.
All she can do now is hope
something else doesn't break again.
God will reach in and pull back baby wearing her first.
Man, forgetting womxn, will say,
that's mine, look at what the Lord has made.
Then after, womxn will be mispronounced.
He said,
it's a boy.
She said,
let the baby decide.
He said,
God damn womxn.

She said,
impossible. Ungrateful man.
It is my emotions that saved you.
Without me, it is unlikely you'd survive.

5.
You are what your mother is.
Therefore, God is a womxn,
the beginning of everything.
Look at what the Lord has made.

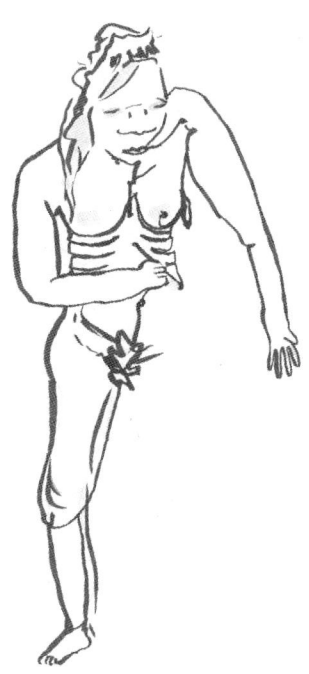

EVE

Rooftop Rendezvous
f/the Caribbean

i brought all my ass to the rooftop we on in tampa
but everything feel like we in brooklyn tha way tha
dj scratching every itch appetizing sounds through
speakers bangin' matching tha way we bounce sweating
bodies dat don stop rollin all over each other do
whateva tha beat say tha ocean in mi panties and only
a few miles away we windin' *hot and groovy in da soca party*
baila with me baby/bam bai dam beh dai/bi dam bem bai bem bai
practicin' everyting tha caribbean sea and sister nancy taught us
slow n steady swift n speedy everybody gettin' what dey asked for
swoonin' n she kiss me like what the fuck is commitment anyway
remembering when two people fell in love on a dance floor for
three minutes and forty seconds but really it's like five minutes
'cause the dj getting high off the way pon di gyals pompasetting
plus he know what to play to make us lose our shit and damn near
come out our clothes stuck like glue move like our ancestors did like
we feelin' to lime bomba unbothered grind ourselves into someting that
fit or you smoke my ass every bit a wave lappin' she ebbin' n flowin' mi
bumpa tha whole scene see us party hard vex vanish the song quit and we
drift away from   each other.

How to Properly Flirt with Someone You're Attracted to and Want to Be Your Boo

AHHHHHHHHHHHHH! Get back over here with my heart!
You smell good.
What is that… forever?

You make me wanna eat my words and spit out my spine.
I'd abandon all my awful for you.
Baby, can I call you baby?
No?

Okay…

You got me blushing in rainbows.
You got me wanting to share the other half of my sandwich.
If we were spiders, I'd web for you,
have a million of your babies,
and then…
eat…
you.
If I were a caterpillar, I'd chew through everything
just to become a butterfly in your stomach.
A chrysalis, I'd break through all this hard for you.

I was an actress once.
A lion tamer, a magician.
I'd stop planning my escape for you.
Stop bad-mouthing love.
Start believing that love is in me and found more of it in you.

You make me wanna figure out
how much wood
would a woodchuck chuck

if a woodchuck could chuck
wood.

When I'm with you, I know that the things that hurt don't have to.
We survivor womyn know how to build walls and make our bodies a fort.
Know how to be survivors of war.
Our expectoration in a constant state of revolution.
Won't you rise with me?
Won't you hip-hop and jazz with me?
Won't you be totally punk rock and scream 'I love you' with me?

When I'm with you, my pulse is a hummingbird.
My body, a parachute
reminding me that I was not meant to live alone
nor is my heart remote from saving.

Can we go through seasons together?
So what if November comes?
I still won't leave or change.
So what if my milkshake brings all the boys to the yard?
You make my heart an adobe home.
Even when they try to earthquake us loose,
I'll be mud brick and hold strong.

You are in a dream I'm having a hundred years from now.
You keep saying you'll be you and allow me to call you mine.

I'd squeeze your pimples or shave your back for you.
You remind me there are easier ways to do things.
I just never took them.

I forget to be afraid when I'm with you.

So I'm sayin' like...
can we be an item or a pair or, like, share space together and stuff?

No?
Okay...

Contacts: Names I Changed Your Name To

Don't Answer. Don't Get Burned Twice By The Same Flame. No Love Allowed. No Fucks Given. Fuck You. Fuck Boi Alert. Ex For A Reason. The Hurter. Satan, I Rebuke You. Donald Trump. Melania Trump. Rachel Dolezal. Christopher Columbus. Napoleon. Batman ('cause he creepy AF). Hannibal Heart Eater. My Mama Don't Like You And She Likes Everyone. *Rolls Eyes* Boogeyman. You'll Cry At The End Of This. Unappreciative Ass. Lyin' Ass. Inconsiderate Ass. Boy Bye. Liar. Cheater. Hitler's Ghosts. Houdini's Stunt Double. The Worst. Shitty Guy. Man, Fuck That Girl. Bye Felicia. I Don't Need You. Snake. Dream Stealer. Now You See Me Now You Don't. Lookin' Ass. DONT DO IT RECONSIDER. Procrastinator. Narcissistic. Avoider. Time Waster.

.

I blocked your number.
You can't call my phone.

Electrolytes

I am in love with a girl I cannot have/that does not want me for keeps. I am in love with a girl who is only temporary or that goes to convenience stores to get milk. A girl who make believes she's coming back/a year later, and we still have nothing to give our bones/still need closure.

I'm in love with a girl whose sorries sound like a Donald Trump speech or a sales pitch. When she calls me beautiful, I know she really mean foolish. She know how to make a vacation out of me. Say my name like she afraid to fall in love. And I know/it's my fault/expecting not to get hurt by a womxn/to take care

of mine the way she would her own. Note to self: loving girls does not keep you from getting hurt by one. Why don't you know this yet? Why haven't you learned? What is lonelier than reminding yourself of what you don't deserve/should not put up with?

I'll tell you/when you see her/love looks away/lust appears as next of kin/whoever is available/whoever picks up the phone and tells you, "you have the wrong number"/even if she calls you back from that number/ready to talk/now/your disposable self/an offering

you accept and regret for days. Later when you think about the scent of your pussy lingering on her fingers/time lapse without remorse or reason. Men aren't the only phantoms/aren't the only ones that don't give an explanation/who take things and don't bring them back/or get whatever good there is to get/leave without having said goodbye. Ghosted—definition—to be ignored or/when a person is moved to another prison without being told in advance. I wonder/when one is ghosted/who then becomes the prisoner or ghost? Is it her and me the spirit/victim? Am I an empty house or casket? Is she the eulogy and me the tears?

Or are we none of these/dependent upon whose poem you read first?

(still waiting...)

I am girl with too many open letters/too much space for forgiveness. Girl with too many ways to get them but can't figure out how to make them stay. Wants something she doesn't have to explain or convince. *And karma says you will fall in love with someone who doesn't love you, for not loving someone who did.* But how the fuck does that even

make sense? Life/an unfair memorial/slut walk/womyn's march/ pride parade/Black lives matter movement. I walk off stage/a spilled gut/an unstitched spine/ one screw from mess/and a man tries to fuck my ears/womxnizing his climax. A lesbian/full of masculinity/ so slick/so deep/she don't even know she persuasive with coercion/ seducing a stereotype/tells me

what she'd do if I were hers/she practically trying to move in wit a nigga. Neither of them really see me past opportunity for conquering. Act like they don't know how long it takes to get over someone. The thirst is real and we're all clearly dehydrated.

I text her saying/it's okay/I'll just drink water.

Today Must Be

Act A Fool, Day.
Break Your Girlfriend's Heart, Day.
Don't Answer The Phone, Day.
Don't Call Back, Day.
Broken Promises, Day.
I Said I Love You, But I Didn't Mean It, Day.
Fuck Boy, Day.
I Say Things I Don't Mean, Day.
I Say Things I Don't Mean So I Can Get What I Want, Day
Say One Thing But Mean Another, Day.
Avoid Life-Making Decisions, Day.
Ruin My Day, Day.
Ruin My Life, Day.
I Don't Need You But I Want You, Day.
I Say Your Name When You're Not Around, Day.

I'll get over it I just gotta be dramatic first

Interlude

In this episode of wanting someone who
did not want me...

I am
being held from behind
by a lover willing to adorn
and pay for my hair weave/
without knowing he is
becoming an expired idol.

Here my dumbass is
hoping my ex is secretly thinking
about   me
like some admirer that know I
exist and plan on surprising me
with them Bruno Mars tickets

'cause/that's/how/a/real/one/come/
back/to claim/they/position and
move from myth to nonfiction.
You know what's weirder than
fantasizing 'bout some shit that'll
never happen?

Admitting you yourself is also on
some fuck boy shit...
Got a whole-ass somebody
who went to college smart enough
to cherish you. Use SAT words and
read books and shit (scientific ones),

too. Even asked you if you seen the

Moon. A whole-ass somebody texted
to see if you was hungry, stayed 'til
morning and told you to "holla if you
need something." Still grab yo ass
and ain't got you wildin'

making you "that crazy bitch" on
the phone or out in public.
Call you back and shit.
A whole-ass somebody paying your
rent and shit. Damn, gurl, you got it
good. Moved out the hood, but you

so grimy you keep jumping
back into a torched house
with fresh flames/begging to be saved
by dudes who only wanna rummage
thru yo goods/but they ain't none.
Heard you lost everything but still

asked to borrow some money.
Here you is,
got the nerve to contemplate
if you should put up with this.
Even yo mama tired of
telling you that THAT nigga

only stick around long enough
to hurt you. You so stupid you
think mamas don't know what
heartbreak feel like/never
getting the last laugh, but
how old was you when yo daddy

left/got kicked out/went off to
war or prison/died? Yo mama
been knowing how to make a

Ebony Stewart

home out of excuses/tears cried.
Gave so many chances, she herself
be more pastor than rapper.

*"Suffering and joy.
A line so thin,
you couldn't have known
the difference."*

Happy Father's Day
the child gets it wrong

he say i only write about the bad things
say i dont remember the good things
say i couldnt know or remember all that bad
said i was too young
guess i got a good imagination
say im still writing about old stuff
guess i aint got over it yet
he dont like how what i write
make him look like
he aint shit
like he aint raise his kids
like he dont love us still
guess i shouldnt write the truth
guess i shouldnt write how i feel
how i grew up
the way i womxn now
guess i shouldnt make him look like he aint nothing
but some sperm donor
some dude
he say he tired of not being the hero in my poems
i say me too
i write what i know
he dont like the memories he left me wit
me neither
dont like being reminded of his faults
but i look in the mirror every day
got his face
what that make me?
i say
how im supposed to escape?
he say im bitter
i say thats what happens when you leave and

aint got nothing when you come back
i say
where im from
that shit hurts
he say i aint gone be successful
i say
you made sure of that
and even if i am
you aint gone have nothing to do with that
either
he say i bought you ice cream once
took you to the movies a few times
made you dinner
played you in Tekken that time
remember?
remember
i came to your volleyball game once
and that one time you played powder puff
remember?
remember
remember i met your boyfriend once
twice
maybe three times
i bought that one book for that one class
while you was in college that one time
came to your wedding
remember we danced
remember?
i was at your graduation
i came to your new house once
remember?
i say/you show up to be seen
to get praise and glory that
dont belong to you.
damn/i must be ungrateful
needing
more than one book

help paying off these student loans
all youve done/shit
guess i shouldnt need for shit
not that shoulder when i got that divorce
when i almost got raped
when i broke my ankle playing those sports
guess i was only hungry once
can watch the same movie for the rest of my life
eat only one flavor of ice cream
but i heard Baskin Robbins got 32
guess i aint need no talkin to on how to get hurt by all these boys
you da bes lesson
guess your hurt is enough for the both of us
you right
i act like you aint do nothing
guess i aint Christian
guess i cant get over it
im so mean
talk to you so bad
treat you so funny
guess when i grew up without you i
took you from me
guess without you id
have nothing to write about
so thank you for teaching me
how to make nothing/out
of
something/the way you raised me

Thank you for letting me go.

On The Way Back To Myself

                Remember when I thought I'd never get over you?
                                      Remember?
                    When I couldn't listen to that song
                          or watch that movie
                          or make that dish
                          or sit in that chair
                          or read that book
                          or go to that place
                      without thinking of you?
            Remember when I thought I'd feel that hurt
                  forever?Couldn't get outta bed.
                  Couldn't keep a smile on my face.

Gurl, look at you now!
You singin whatever song you got.
Dancin.
Movin.
Showin all yo teeth!
Knowin your *body is not an apology*.
Ain't nobody *runnin away with all yo stuff*.
Yo whole presence holy.
Shiiiit, BLESS UP!
You whimsical and delicate as fuck.
You smart as fuck.
Yo pussy magic, and you know it,
etcétera etcétera etcétera
                    AS FUCK.
You ain't gotta stay nowhere,
or wit nobody,
that don't appreciate you
        or whatevah.

You healthy and shit.
Drinkin water and shit.
Still got love to give yourself and shit.
Made time to wash your whole body clean.
Co-washed the fuck outta them emotions.
Gurl, you coconut oil saved and moisturized.
Somebody said what about you?
Gurl, boo.
Them niggas hatin.
Somebody ain't want you?
Boy, bye.
Them niggas MUST BE mistaken.
We woke up this morning AMAZING.
Gone go to sleep STARGAZING.
Soft when I wanna be.
Hard when I have to be.
Girl, you yo own Aaliyah 4 Page Letter.
You Missy Elliott Supa Dupa Fly.
What cho credit score is?
Bitch, we ain't even in the same tax bracket,
                        you can't talk to me.
I'm so valuable.
I. Do. What. I. Want.
We gully for a reason.
Southern for a reason.
Still live in the south,
while you went away,
but all my southern back talk still live where I stay.
SHOUT OUT TO ALL MY EDGES STILL BABY HAIR LAID.
Tears for what?
If it ain't joy, we don't want it.
If it ain't glee, we can't keep it.
Na, excuse me, while I put back into myself,
all that attention I been needin.

I Am
(after Monica Hand)

I am
a. what you say I am or what I answer to. some of us carry our prison with us wherever we go.
b. cell memory. same family. different colors.
c. water mixed with blood; call us mud babies; a thicker version of war, race, and freedom.
d. mashed berries, sugar cane, and stewed fruit. a boiling mixture. some parts sweeter than others/an acquired taste.
e. all of the above.
          WE ranked in order of importance
The white man by default. Writer of the best seller/teller of the number one lie/got us believing womxn came from his ribs/and/'cause his ribs white/then come the white womxn/i.e., the most protected, the most beautiful, better than, greater than, the most important. In conclusion: light is always right, is always valued, is always loved, is always wanted. Me/dark skin Black womxn. 3 strikes. So she be wrong/ain't got the answers to none of these white…I mean, right questions. It's not a problem as long as I don't look up, don't move forward, don't want for nothing more than what I've been taught, or been given. Gotta keep believin' I can only be the holy ghost or spirit but never a God.
so, I fantasized a river. dreamed it had a beautiful flow. gave to it all of me/and to all of me it gave. but when I awoke, now when I go to dip my toe in the creek, to bathe, play, or drink, all my children be dammed, from taking on too much of somebody else's shit/be blocked fools/keep expecting to be healthy while drinking from a cesspool. you know some say we too dense to float. but my great grand made a boat out of her mouth/splintered and stretched into groove, into gully, into gulf.
so where did I come from?
a. Big Mama. a stowaway on a ship to Carencro. a dry land tourist or c'est un nouveau pour moi or should I call where I am, home?

b. a reservoir. a fancy word for suppressing floods. the overflow of emotions. coming as one, leaving as many.
c. the block in my own flow/an interruption in greatness. or sometimes when you think you drownin all you gotta do is stand up.
d. bits and pieces of a story told from a larger body. chanting: we are not what has tried to kill us/we are always what learns to survive *what refuses to die.*
e. all of the above

What We Become
pick a metaphor

The tree.
The fruit.
The grass.
The street.
The flowers.

The soil.
The blood.
The blood.
Blood.
And blood.

The gun.
The bullet.
The dog.
The prison.
The hanging.

The mother.
The tears.
The black suit.
The casket.
The funeral.

The anger.
The outrage.
Printed.
Broadcasted.
The news.

The murder.
The song.

The poem.
The rant.
A hashtag.

Gone too soon.

She could've been me.
That could've been you.
_____ and _____
is me, too.

The graveyard.
The thug.
The Skittles.
The hoodie.
The threat.
The sit-ins.
The boycotts.
The silent protest.
The movement.
A knee.

The evil.
The bad.
The stupid.
The dumb.
A narrative.

Magic is for make-believe.

The lesson.
The rhyme.
The riddle.
The example.
The joke.

The monkey.

The ape.
The spook.
The coon.
A nigger.

The ....
And the ....
No remorse or regret.

But my favorite kind is the one where they put us in nursery rhymes
so at least it sounds like we got to be alive and live a life we could fully enjoy,

> "All around the mulberry bush.
> The monkey chased the weasel.
> The monkey thought t'was all in fun.
> Then POP! goes the weasel."

I got some friends Black when it's convenient.

Not the race, but the color.
'Cause if you dark skin,
everybody know you less fortunate.
"Because, like, I wanna be Black
but I really don't wanna BE Black."[2]
But Beyonce get to claim a ward
and didn't grow up in no hood/
ain't attend public school.
Praise Beyonce 'cause she made it.
Praise Beyonce 'cause she beautiful
and everything say she prettier than me.
Praise the bees that follow that swarm.
Watch them sting all the black on me.
But bruises only show up on light skin girls.
Praise the light skin girls who Black
but call themselves brown.
'Cause who wanna be Black anyhow?
Not the race, but the color.
I got some brown skin cousins woke as fuck
but keep the language of our oppressors as
a back hand/identity. 'Cause everything say
she better than me and chosen first.
When they say more womyn of color are
now being seen or heard—I know
they ain't talking about me.
Not the race, but the color.
I wonder, when will God ever look like or at me?
When will my pain ever be described as more than

---

2   LaLove Robinson

brave or necessary? How did I get this strong? Or chosen to die for all our sins? Blood lent to someone else's body. Colorism so deep we got hatred perfect.

Re-Conditioning

> *"Where there is a womxn there is magic."* –Ntozake Shange

My friend Mandy say I got that good hair. Say she used to pray that one day she'd have hair like mine. And all of a sudden we are another difference society makes of us. She wanna know how my hair got this way, and I'm defensive/as if I didn't come like this. Unaware that a slightly unfurled fist still be considered to have the upperhand. Like ain't no such thing as textural privilege. Like we both just get to be some carefree Black girls/hair blowing in the wind. But ask any soufflé, curl-maker, eco-styler, castor-oil, flaxseed, avocado, or edge-control and it'll call me a liar/leader of this church where I religiously worship/lay my burdens down but dare not come as I am. Call me grown womxn still learning what cocktail bring me closer to a coil, wave, or curl pattern I can call a miracle or at least consider myself poppin'. Fingers still figuring out how to work with a natural texture growing from my own scalp. A head that's been with me since I was born. My hair be shame and the baby of the family. Taught early-on how to be less girl and more chemically altered/not even I should have to put up with myself. Who else is embarrassed but won't admit they too had to watch a video clip to be educated on all the ways our hair can be manipulated? Got all this hairitage without endurance—'cause a 2 or 3 strand twist, crochet, braid, or perm rod make my wrist burn, my neck sore, and lower back ache. Praise the wash-and-go tutorials that teach me to submerge my hair/and be a holy baptism or oblation of autonomy. But we still feel the need to stretch and length-check to debunk the myth that Black hair don't grow. Still feel the need to make a 2A, 3B, 4ABC hair type/villain out of each other. Like being Black womyn in America ain't hard enough. Like Black men won't cheat/still not know how to love us wild and untamed/without calling us nappy-headed when they're tired of us.

I say, girl, we all got good hair/as in strong, of quality and resilience/righteously worshiping at the congregation of porosity where we are learning to wash, deep-condition, and grow.

Slapboxing
Not just another hood game

Slapboxing
"is a physical activity somewhat simulating boxing, where open hands are used in lieu of fisticuffs."[3] The art form is "an intersection between sparring and fighting usually performed in an informal manner," the hood, the bus stop, the park, on yo block where there's no vaseline but still two young men (some niggas) squarin' off, talkin' trash, wit a hard gaze.

Think of it as a tool to be used to test one's hand speed and power.
Where males show dominance over each other.
i.e., who has the longest reach, the quickest hands,
who can bob and weave, block and move forward,
all while showboating and being the most flamboyant.

A rite of passage if you will.
Little brother finally defeats and connects with older brother to gain his respect.

Aggression used as an outlet when one cannot otherwise communicate their feelings.

A spontaneous game or training drill between acquaintances
that never lasts more than a couple of minutes
because 120 seconds is actually a really long time
and usually ends from a really good hit
a.k.a. "That nigga hit me too hard and now we 'bout to fight for real."
a.k.a. how else is a Black man allowed to express himself in anger, when being tempered still get red confetti slung from his body?
or

---

3   Slapboxing - Wikipedia

name a Black man that hasn't squared up daily
with his white opponent and lost—
not because of skill, velocity, reach, or endurance,
but because white men break the rules when Black men get the best of
them. (i.e., George Zimmerman, Timothy Loehmann,
Michael Dunn, Donald Trump, ...) *(white men, white men,
white men, ...)* Crumble under pressure, only slapbox those
they know they can beat
by bringing a knife or a gun to a fight that only requires the use of hands.
Name a coward that didn't break the rules, make a fist, a bomb, a "law",
and hit a nigga hard enough for the ground to open up and fit a
whole body in. Or at the very least, didn't send the police mob
to our neighborhoods with maximum power and chains.

The one who gets the most licks wins the game.
And some of this country's greatest slapboxers
(i.e., Nat Turner, Malcolm X,
James Baldwin, Muhammad Ali, Jackie Robinson, Chuck Berry,
Eric Garner, Sandra Bland, ...) said, "I know my rights and you
can get these hands" got the most licks, is legends in these streets/
but was born defeated/dusted and given a tombstone for it.

Remember half-swings are wasted energy.

Develop an eye for what's coming.

The idea is to strike your opponent without them striking you.

Stick. Move. Block.
The blindspot to this strategy of revenge, escape, or attempt to not
be erased is:

white men never intend to use just their hands.

Compassion Fatigue

To the white womxn whose YouTube comment said
she is tired of every other American poem being about race or rape.
I'm not sure if compassion fatigue happens
because no one taught you how not to be oppressed
or because no one taught you how not to be the oppressor,
but your comment reminds us that *no one cares about us but us.* [4]
You're right. There are no new topics,
just old problems written into new pleas
to a country that refuses to reckon with its own sickness.
We Americans,
land of the free,
can only keep our motto
if we keep our mouths closed. And isn't that what all rapists want?
Control and a silenced victim.
Do you realize someone has stopped listening to this poem
because I am first Black and also a womxn? Black, if I'm alive still.
Womxn, if I haven't disappeared yet.
Got anything anybody in the world might need
except my voice—
which means,
my body must be what's left for the taking.
I'm not sure how we became *treasures we can't afford to keep.*
But there are womyn of all kinds who've been raped;
who also hoped their warm bodies' heart would stop beating,
but still went to work the next day.
What we know is,
it's hard to comfort a girl who doesn't let on she's hurting.
So praise every womxn who speaks out against her rapist in an effort
to heal.
Praise the ones who didn't,
but got their healing from the poems you are tired of hearing.

---

[4] "Liliane" by Ntozake Shange

How easy it must be to only sit through the happy.
While we try an' believe the only thing we need to remember
about suffering is that,
eventually,
it ends.
Three times now, on social media, I've watched a Black person be murdered
because the United States is still making us pay for the way we look
or the guilt it feels.
But a person of color's only glory hallelujah is
as long as we didn't die, then we didn't die.
Do you realize
that when our mothers say, "I love you,"
she is also saying,
stay alive,
come back to me whole, in one piece,
and not a hashtag
or another dead *nigga* whose death she'll have to watch on repeat?
Us poets,
whose duty is to write about the times,
write, because we don't know when we'll become extinct.
We are what's left.
Black ink from Black poets, who dare to respond to all this Black
death, instead of hiding behind everything we're thinking.
How privileged your life must be,
that you can be tired of hearing poems about race or rape,
while we write about an extinguished race
and violated bodies that keep being raped.

It's not hard to believe you're tired,
but can you empathize with how exhausted
we
must
be?

Perhaps we should go back.

Pack our suitcases, boxes, and barrels full of:
rice, sugar, and cotton
spices, recipes, and oils
ancestry, legacy, and midnight
customs, greetings, and slang
our melanin and our organs
music, moods, and memes
photographs, language, and plunder
witchery, Black magic, and holistics
unruly, offensive, good for nothing
but dying, twice as good, bodies.

Leave them to their
pale and soleless
selfish and greedy, offbeat selves
weathered and rubber faces
unseasoned chicken and Kardashians
winter womyn without legs
love for hatred, conniving and conning
their obsession with murder and war
raping and killing
injustices and prisons
dick-measuring politics.

I say we leave.
Start our own government
without their obstacles and struggle
America and its robbery.
Name ourselves as Gods
delivered from everything.
Be original, jubilee, tribe and kin.
Use the rest of our time left loving and

undoing the anguish done to us by their men.
Be our own unique and beautiful.
Leave them dullard, ugly, and terrible.
Let them rot with nothing
unable to survive without us.

Let them not forget that this
is the reason we were summoned.
A whole illusion of weak people pretending
to be white/claiming to have superiority.
but unable/unfit/remiss to do anything.

Family Tree

In this family/where all the brothers die before their sisters. Where the womyn still fix the men their plates. Where patriarchy got its own vein. Where the boys who weren't allowed to cry/are now men with wild emotions. Who'll be right back/who take too long/who think they can do whatever they want/who buy slabs and jam screw/who hella homophobic/and can tell me what the Bible say/but contradict/ themselves just like the God they created/who know how to do the right thing/they just ain't always interested in it/who get locked up/ who write letters/who get visits and ask for scriptures and bail money/and still drink 40s/and listen to oldies/and don't say I love you (too much)/who got high blood pressure and diabetes/and cheat on they old ladies/but still say, "Go ask yo mama." Because the matriarchs run everything.

Yes, these men/
come from this family.

The same family where/we got multiple baby mamas/three baby daddies/and hold on to our children. And we be mommas baby/ forevah/even when she put us out/and beg us to come back. We burn everything we cook for flavor & call it Cajun. Granny say, don't marry for love, marry for support (in both languages). We do not come in and out of the house. Learned early on to make decisions and live with the consequences. We say to our pain, "drink some water" "walk it off" "go to sleep" and "you okay." To our cuts, bruises, and booboos, "lemme see" "put some spit on it" "drink some water" "walk it off" "go to sleep" and "you ain't dead" "you okay." We dramatic as fuck, but we do not go to counseling/we don't always know how to talk about it/if we talk about it. We pray for everything and over everything. Even my dead Grandmothers are tired. Even our God in heaven/is tired.

We go to Church. Wear "play clothes"/and square up/and talk loud/ and walk hard/and can be mean. And "I SAID WHAT I SAID" /and don't apologize/'cause we shouldn't have to apologize. We only think of what someone did to us. We remember what someone did to us. We close doors at night so we can hear what's trying to come for us. We wear sneakers but ain't never running from nothing. We carry guns and wish a nigga would, so we can pop something.

We know how to drop a whole ass to the floor and clap it back up/'cause we only middle-class ghetto fabulous. We/play dominos and know what you got in yo hand. We/play spades and will fight/if you play the wrong card/or lie on yo hand/and fuck up how many books we said we could get. We stop talking for years. We can suck our teeth and roll our eyes for days. We ain't said nothing/but you can see it all over our face. We braid hair on the porch/in the backyard/in the living room/in the bathroom/in sis bedroom with a pillow under us. That tumbleweave came from my house.

We laugh hearty and long and split something. We give, but not always our last/'cause we gotta keep something in case you don't remember to pay us back. We got gas money. We got a light bill in somebody else's name. We don't complain. We get it how we live. Some of us is the reason we can't have nice things. We all got diplomas/some of us degrees/but ain't none of us no dummies.

This family/a tree/a heartbeat/a limb—girl you can't date him,
that's yo cousin.

Fear

I am asked to write about the birth of my demons.
To tell how fear is born, the way it came into existence.
I struggle myself to ink, strike through words,
crumble a hundred pages with FEAR written all over them.
Leaving me waist deep in torture.
Feel the blood lap itself under my skin.
Flood my body with every story that has ever consumed me.
Fear, must've been born like this—in tremble and strange sounds.
Must be a belly's echo with muffled screams slung all around.
Must be an artist.
Must be an international student
relearning everything that couldn't make its way across the ocean.
Fear must be an island.
Must be lonely growing lusciously.
Must've grown fangs and thorns and vines.
Must've wrapped itself in everything hard and hurt.
Must've strangled love until its eyes popped out.
Fear must be blind and touching everything.
Fear must have eight arms and three heads.
Must be a monster mating with itself multiple times
until it became a forest, a continent, a whole person, a place to live.
Fear must have a stubborn heart.
Must thump stress, speak creep, must haunt
your dreams, your goals, your happiness.
Fear be a bottom feeder, must scrape every last bit
of hope from your feet, must keep you stuck and graduated hater.
Yeah, fear must be a cowboy roping, hanging.
It must be a gangster with a machine gun, must be a police officer
with an empty weapon after emptying his weapon inside the soul of
a Black body.
It must be a Black mother's home with all these unarmed Black
bodies walking around.

Fear must be a nigga. And *everybody wanna be a nigga, but don't nobody wanna be a nigga.*
Shots fired. Yeah. Shots fired.
Yeah, fear must be balmy, coiled, beauty, and exotic.
The only person of color in the whole room.
Fear must be the revolution untelevised.
Must be a man calling out another man when misogyny forces its way into his mouth.
Fear must be coming out but, still having to pretend to be someone else.
Must be a body in transition.
Must be permission for two womyn to kiss in public
for two men to hold hands.
Fear must be given.
Must be a law, must be in place to save the human race.
Quote, "The universe wrote fiction in us; it's called fear."[5]
And I'm not saying I'm ashamed.
I don't even wanna be brave.
I just don't wanna be afraid to be myself.
But fear is the part of me I know the most.
Therefore, I think I'm free, but am I really?

Fear is who we loving, sexing, and paying our tithes too.
Yes!
Fear is a god.
A religion.
Who we pray to.
And believe in.

Fear mustn't be uttered, admitted, or claimed to have faith in.
Fear must just be who fear be and how fear came about.

---

5   Christopher Poindexter

I Love Mondays

I myself was born at 3:45am.
I took my first breath on a Monday.
I never understood why people hate Mondays.
Have you heard the way people talk about Mondays?

> *Oh crap, tomorrow's Monday!*
> *Looks like someone's got a case of the Mondays.*

Monday is the first of the five obstacles you must pass before
reaching the glorified weekend!
People hate Mondays the same way they hate niggas and Muslims.
Fucking Mondays.

As if Monday did something to you
as if it's Monday's fault you gotta go to work
as if it's Monday's fault you hate your job or
that the government don't pay you enough
to wake up on a Monday or that society has you thinking
your worth is from 9 to 5, 40 hours, 5 days a week
as if it's Mondays fault Sunday is your only day of rest.

Why don't people hate Sundays?

I mean, after all, Sunday is the reason why Monday sucks, right?
Sunday reminds you of what will always come to an end.
Sunday is the day that ends its praise by giving up.
It's Monday and somebody didn't wake up this morning.
It's Monday and a mother has only one week to plan her child's
funeral, his father's funeral, our grandmother's funeral.
Every day is Monday when you wake up alive.
Every day is Sunday when you learn to operate in forgiveness.

And so bless every day you get to breathe, you get to take a breath.
Praise every day that teaches us about surviving again and again—especially on Mondays.

I think if I ever have a child, I'ma name it Monday.
The day after Sunday—after holy, came you.
I had to think about you before you came.
I had to make plans.
You were how I started and rearranged, how I make sure things end well.
Monday, people are going to say mean things about you.
Not gonna welcome you with open arms.
Not gone want you to come around.
It'll feel like the whole world is against you.
But if you weren't you, they'd just hate Tuesday
And then Wednesday, until all yo kinfolk is gone.

People will always want someone or something to blame, Monday.

It just happens to be you—a day after everything had been sacrificed; they still want something more from you.
They'll only want you if you're temporary
if you give them something good—like a holiday
a barbecue, a patch of grass. You gotta work so much harder than every other day to be green, to be new.
Monday, I know you can do it; you've done it before.

I was born on a Monday.
Monday at 3:45am.

I took my first [breath].

Black womyn be wanting to stop & cry so badly, but there's shit to do.

Happy Mother's Day

My mother is the kind of womxn who, when she's angry, her voice goes from an impatient car horn to a tornado siren.

My mother is the kind of womxn who, when she hits you, she tryin to knock your head from your shoulders, your teeth loose, eyeballs crooked.

The kind of womxn who, if she didn't like your answer to why you did something, would send you back to your room—the one she took the door off its hinges so couldn't slam it/cause you don't own nothing in this house/so you can think of a better answer. Who say, "look at me when I'm talking to you" and "you bettah fix yo face" and "stop cryin before I give you something to cry about." As if she didn't—when she always did.

One time she blew the wind so hard she picked up the whole house/so we could know just how much to her there was.

Take a knife/a fork/a shoe/a comb/pop you quick, jig you quick, remind you real quick who yo mama was when she ain't to be played with.

But all your friends think your mama is SO SWEET.

Swear my mama was a wrestler in her former life the way she make us tap out.

Or some baseball legend the way she aim with precision.

My mother is the kind of womxn whose only justification is "because I said so!"

Love us so much her whole body is a window bar and security gate. Protect us like—ain't nobody gettin in.

The kind of womxn who did it on her own/sacrificed everything. We didn't need for nothing/never knew we didn't have nothin, 'cause we had everything.

The kind of womxn that when she come home from work, she don't wanna hear nothing about our problems especially if they start with the silliest: "I want…" and "I need…"

To which she'd reply: "you wanna leave me alone" and "you need to read

a book" or "bring me your homework so I can see what you been doing all day."
The kind of womxn who worried herself with the details but never once told us about the details/let them kids be kids.
The kind of kids that if she cooked it you gone eat it or you gone sit there in the same spot all night until she tired of you looking at it.
The kind of womxn who want her kitchen cleaned and clothes folded before the morning 'cause somehow it helped her sleep better.
The same womxn who'll wake up to wake you up to yell and swing her hands, "ya'll better get cho A-S-S-es up and clean my damn kitchen!"
"I like yo nerves. You ain't THAT sleep!" Even if we were. Even if she didn't. Dirty kitchens wake my mama out her sleep.
The kind of womxn you bet not ask to go nowhere Saturday night til her whole house is clean Saturday morning. Magic 102 on the radio/Luther Vandross on the radio/Johnnie Taylor on the radio/Zydeco on the radio.
My mama, some Southern gospel she is/as she wanna be
mix Jamaican slang without knowin/ain't a place Western Culture ain't invaded/no war without blood/no roti that ain't gumbo/no dish without fish/ without rice/no body without song/singing ["You got the wrong bum bum"]
No wonder
she make breaking sound like laughter,
make a whisper sound like a Sunday morning prayer.
Fold her fingers to fix, forgive, and heal anything.
This is how my mother taught us survival.
This is why my mother is also a survivor.
My mother keep the Moon in her eyes/so everything is an ocean and I am her sky.
I learned the ways of her waves, her ripple/and mimic her sea.
And so I pray to God, if I ever have children, my mother is the kind of mother I wanna be.

I'M SO TIRED...
the anthem

of writing or reading about everything I ain't,
couldn't be, or what happened to me. FUCK
that shit! Today, I'M THAT BITCH YOU LOVE
TO HATE! The one you say, she is
smart, she is kind, she is important, and
that shit makes you sick, don't it? I'm
Cardi B's tongue out. I'm Viola Davis,
Taraji P. Henson, and Badu. Which is to say,
I got babies wit some of these niggas.
My feet hurt and I'm too cute to
dance anyway. I'm so extra I'm Teyana Taylor.
I sweated out a blowout
dancing like my hair don't poof.
I'm 4 bundles—the expensive kind. I'm crochet,
box braids, and Senegalese twist—the poppin' kind.
I'm Saturday night at Pappadeaux's—the one where
all the Black people go/'cause I'm fancy
and frugal as fuck. I made eye contact
just so you could see me not speak.
She who kept her booty the size it came in.
She who made it clap harmoniously. Taught white
girls how to twerk. Do you know how long
it takes to teach white girls how to twerk?
Or to do...anything? Bitch, I invented rhythm.
I don't know none of the words to the national anthem.
I'm Nina Simone when she stopped her own song
and told that girl to sit down. Have
a million seats. I roll my eyes
when you talk. Matter fact, my superpower
I can look you dead in the face
while you're talkin and not hear
a damn word you said. I don't waste
energy on what you THINK.

I don't even use that word.
'Cause womyn like me give birth to
Nelson Rogers & Big Freedia 'cause
YOU ALREADY KNOOOOWWW!
I took yo man cause he belong to everybody.
Exposed all his fuck shit and you
still took him back. Do better sis.
I'll be over here reclaiming my time. And
*I'd tell you what I don't have time for
but I don't have time.*[6] I got
hot sauce and hand grenades in my bag.
I'm the church lady in the front row
wit the big hat, who caught the holy ghost
cause I couldn't hold my mule. The one
who's saved and sanctified, but you can still
get these hands. 'Cause I love God & trap
music. I wanna 'pologize, but I'm not really
sorry. #iwokeuplikethis #whogonecheckmeboo
It's the return of the burn/I thought you knew.

---

6   "Gravity" by Angel Nafis

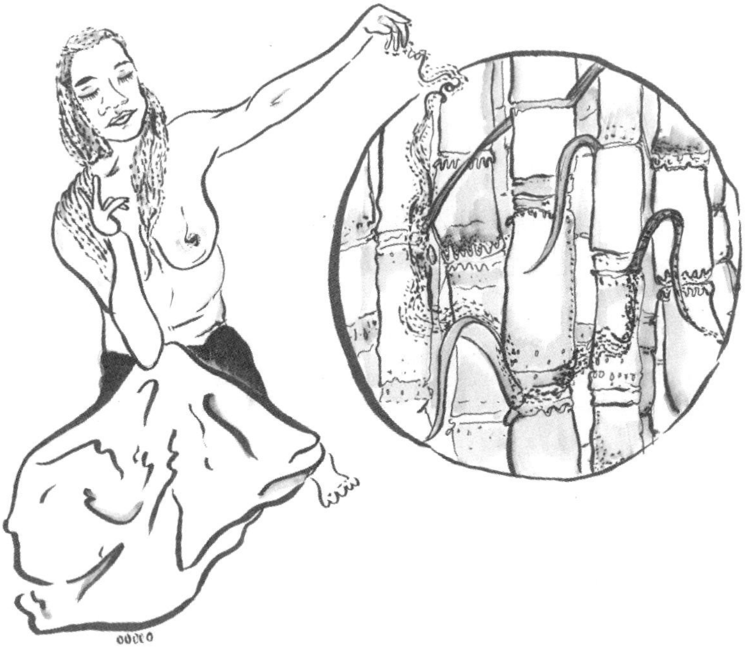

button poetry

To access and learn more about the *Home.Girl.Hood.* curriculum as a resource for your classroom, home schooling, and workshops or to review and purchase samples of the Deluxe or PG version in Common Core or Texas TEKS, please visit EbPoetry.com or Teachers Pay Teachers.com/Store/Ebpoetry.

I Am (pp. 38–39)

Key Terms	• **c'est un nouveau pour moi**: this is new to me • **Carencro**: a small city in Louisiana • **empowerment**: the act of granting authority, power, or right to someone or something • **identity**: the distinguishing character or personality of someone • **intersectionality**: the complex way the effects of multiple forms of discrimination (for example, classism, racism, and sexism) combine, or overlap, especially in the experiences of marginalized individuals or groups • **reclamation**: the act of rescuing from improper use • **womxn**: a variation of the word "women" used in feminist contexts to avoid the word ending in "men" and to be inclusive of transgender women
Literary Terms and Devices	• **list poem**: a list or inventory of ideas, items, people, places, or words that may use repetition and does not necessarily need to rhyme • **structure**: the way the text of the poem is presented to the reader • **word bank**: a list of words relating to the material at hand
Materials	• "I Am" by Ebony Stewart • "Freedom speaks" by Monica Hand • Audio and video projection of a YouTube video • Paper and pencil, or computer, to write • Presentation paper

Duration	45 minutes

Warm-Up: Starting a Word Bank (5 minutes)
- Have the students write seven words of how close family and friends would describe them.
- Then, have the students write seven words of how they would describe themselves.
- Finally, have the students perform their adjectives and have the class guess what the adjective is. As students are guessing correctly, collect those words on a presentation paper, titled Word Bank, for all to see.

Considerations for Teacher: In this poem, students create a poem about their multiple identities. They also explore how these identities are often undervalued or put down by society.

Consider participating in what is asked of the students. This simple act helps model the exercise, sharpen students' ideas, and ultimately help build trust with students.

Part One: "I Am" (20 minutes)

- Have students spend less than five minutes reading "I Am"
  - Have multiple students read the poem "I Am" aloud, one at a time.
  - As a closer listening exercise, have students write a quote, question, and/or comment as they listen to the poem being read.
- Play the video for "I Am" (https://youtu.be/6n01ZiNPzcA)

Discussion Questions:
Response

- What are your initial reactions to the poem?
- How did the performance of the poem differ from how you read it? How was it similar?

Style
- How would you describe the format of the poem? What does that format convey to you?

Content

- **Empowerment** is the act of granting authority, power, or right to someone or something. In what ways is the poem "I Am" about empowerment? Who or what is being empowered? With what are they being empowered?
- **Identity** is the distinguishing character or personality of someone. In what ways is the poem "I Am" about identity?
- **Intersectionality** is the complex way the effects of multiple forms of discrimination (for example, classism, racism, and sexism) combine, or overlap, especially in the experiences of marginalized individuals or groups. In what ways does this poem address intersectionality?
- **Reclamation** is the act of rescuing from improper use. In what ways is this poem about reclamation? Who or what is being reclaimed?
- How might the gender, race, and age of the author, Ebony Stewart, influence the reading of the poem "I Am"?
- What does she mean in the line "keep expecting to be healthy while drinking from a cesspool."?
- What words in this poem strike you as particularly descriptive of the poet?

Part Two: "I Am" (20 minutes)

- Ask students what are words the world would use to describe them. Generate a new, second word bank on a second presentation paper.
- Compare and contrast this new word bank to the words the students wrote in the first word bank during the Warm-Up.
- Ask the students to write a list poem about their identity. Have them consider their various intersections.

- After 10–15 minutes (or as appropriate), ask for volunteers to share their writing. Then, request constructive feedback from the students for each read poem.

Conclusion: Have all students turn in a copy of their work for teacher review. Constructive feedback should be given and returned to them for next drafts.

> **Differentiated Instruction:**
>
> **Extension:** Have the class read "Freedom speaks" by Monica Hand.
> - Ask "Would anyone like to read this aloud?"
>
> **Response**
> - What are your initial reactions to the poem?
> - How did "Freedom speaks" make you feel?
>
> **Style**
> - What does the format of the poem remind you of?
>
> **Content**
> - How are the poems "Freedom speaks" by Monica Hand and "I Am" by Ebony Stewart similar?
> - How are the poems different?

Fear (pp. 55–56)

Key Terms	• **misogyny**: a hatred of women • **phobia**: an exaggerated, illogical, and inexplicable of something • **womyn**: a variation of the word "women" used in feminist contexts to avoid the word ending in "men"
Literary Terms and Devices	• **personification**: the representation of something with human qualities • **perspective**: a mental view which serves as a lens through which readers observe characters, events, and happenings • **repetition**: the use of repeating a word or phrase several times to make the idea clearer or more memorable
Materials	• "Fear" by Ebony Stewart • Paper and pencil, or computer, to write
Duration	45 minutes

Warm-Up: Discussion (5 minutes)
What is fear?
- What are some things to be afraid of or to fear?
- What are examples of cultural fears?
- What are examples of irrational fears?
- What are examples of environmental fears?
- A **phobia** is an exaggerated, illogical, and inexplicable of something. What are examples of phobia?
  - What are you afraid of?
  - Is fear a weakness?
  - What does fear feel like?
  - How can you overcome fear?
  - How does it feel to overcome fear?

Considerations for Teacher: This conversation should encourage participants to feel vulnerable, and also to see the value and growth fear offers.

Part One: "Fear" (20 minutes)
- Have students spend less than five minutes reading "Fear"
  - Ask "Would anyone like to read this aloud?"

Discussion Questions:
Response
- What are your initial reactions to the poem?

Style
- What are examples of repetition in this poem? How does the repetition impact the reading?
  - What are examples of personification in this poem?
  - Why are there multiple personifications of fear in this poem?

Content
- In the fourth line ("Crumble a hundred pages with FEAR written all over them."), what impact does the all-caps spelling of FEAR have on the reading?
- What does she mean in the line "Must be a belly's echo with muffled screams slung all around."?
- Does the poet reject fear? Embrace fear? Overcome fear? Why or why not?

Part Two: "Fear Personified" (20 minutes)
- Have students write their own "Fear" poems personifying fear.
- Describe different life phases of the personification
    of fear, including,
    - Birth
    - Upbringing
    - Death
- Stress the impact of repetition in their poem, as it also creates a rhythm for the writer.
- After 10–15 minutes (or as appropriate), ask for volunteers to share their writing. Then, request constructive feedback from the students for each read poem.

Conclusion: Have all students turn in a copy of their work for teacher review. Constructive feedback should be given and returned to them for next drafts.

Differentiated Instruction:
- **Interpersonal**: Challenge interpersonal learners to write a poem about someone else's fear in the second-person perspective.
- **Logical-Mathematical**: Challenge logical-mathematical learners to create a timeline of the life phases of the personification of fear.

Extension: This poem, "Fear", quotes a poem by Christopher Poindexter from his "The Universe and Her, and I" series of short poems. Have students research this project and select their favorite poems from this series. Then, ask students to share their favorites aloud.
- What did you like about the poem?
- Why did it speak to you?
- What are the commonalities between all the shared poems?
- What are the differences?

Poems from *Home.Girl.Hood.* available for download in alternative languages available on EbPoetry.com

German
I Love Monday's
How to Properly Flirt
Eve
Happy Father's Day

Italian
Compassion Fatigue
I Love Monday's

Spanish
Hairitage
How to Properly Flirt
Compassion Fatigue
Happy Father's Day
Happy Mother's Day

Yugoslavian
Hairitage
Compassion Fatigue

Shoutouts

My mama love me so much she pray for my success and God listens to her. She see me when ya'll don't. She feed me with all kinds of Southern Jamerican dishes. We traded places, this time I get to be the daughter and she the mother. We are best friends. Thank you for the womyn we have become.

Shoutout to Ariana Brown and Michael Whalen, ya'll keep me grammatically correct, better, and punctuated. I ask for more than I could ever repay. Thank you for your patience.

Shoutout to Write About Now Poetry Slam & Timber Mouse Publishing for once being HGH's home. Thank you to the Houston and Austin, Texas slam fam & spoken word community. Thank you for always rooting for me and acknowledging my work as enough.

I've had the same best friend since I started liking people, so shoutout to Jennifer Gray for speaking my language.

Shoutout to Dr. Angel L. Wilson, my sisterfriend and teacher. I don't deserve you.

Professor Paul Cohen, *till you do right by me*, I'mma keep writing just to prove you wrong.

Through it all, be it sadness, laughter, tears, anger, defeat, awards, a hug, a meal, a phone call, text message, a night out, a drink, DM, a couch, a bed, friendship, loyalty, consistency, and I ain't neva gotta wonder what I mean to you:

Peg Gavin, April Neal, Ebo Barton, Jon Goode, The VORTEX, Pages Matam, Yöeme Hömari, King Wāni, RaShea Bell, Dallas Poetry Slam, Taji SeniorGipson, Kirsche Dickson, Lizz Lewis, Central Michigan University, Oom Pa, Michael Lee Wolf, Adam Maurer, BedPost Confessions, Sonja Parks, Lindsey Ervi, Hieu Minh Nguyen, Jessica Molina, Fatima Mann, Te'aunna Moore, Sharon Bridgforth, Dr. Joni Jones, Toronto Poetry Slam, Alice Chipkin, Melbourne Poetry Slam, CeCe Jordan, Justin Smith, Cindy Stewart, Daddy Gray, Ebony Payne, Sasha Banks, Whitney Weathersby, Angie Hodge, Trena Saunders, Natasha T. Miller, Bookwomxn, Marlon Hall & Folklore Films.

Shoutout to those who celebrate me, who don't know me but send me messages just to tell me that they love me and my work helped keep them alive today... you kept me alive today too.

Shoutout to my ancestors, God, Yahweh, Universe, Yemayá, and She. I am nothing without the divinity of who you've made me and who you keep helping me to be. Thank you that when they see me, they see you, when they hear me, they hear you, when they feel me, they feel you -- and I am strong, empowering, uplifted, relatable, and undeniably enough.

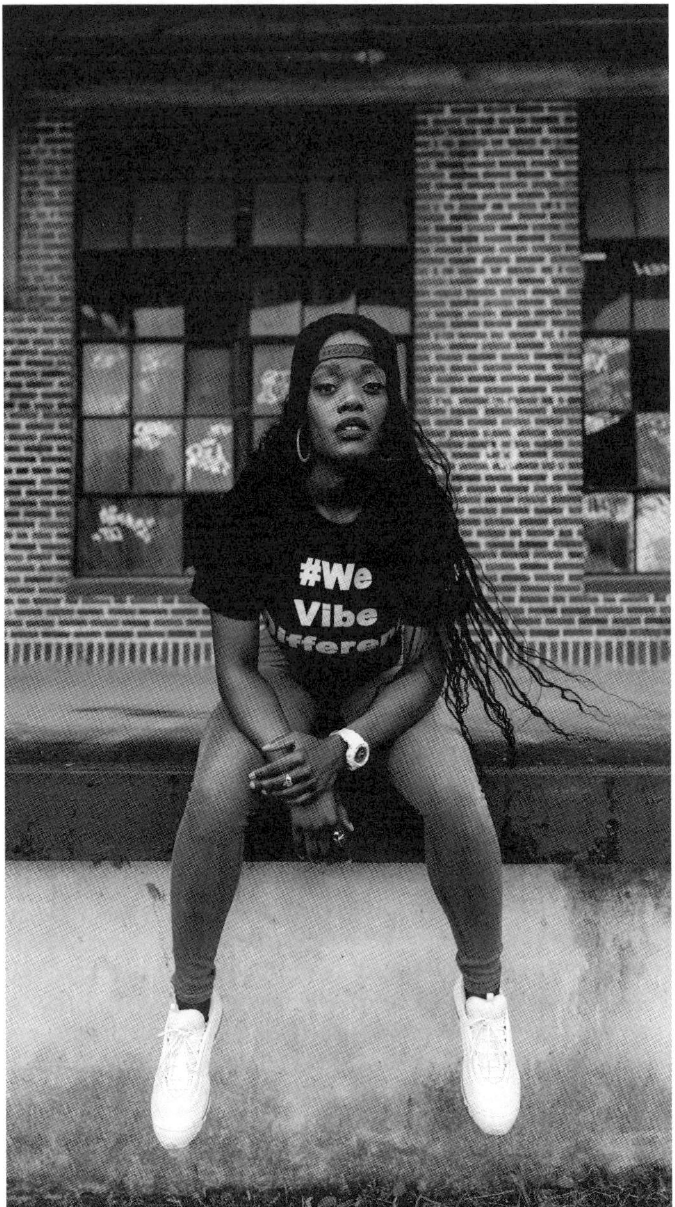
#We
Vibe

Ebony Stewart is an international touring performance artist, spoken word artist, and playwright. The 2017 Womyn of the World Poetry Slam Co-Champion. The only adult female three-time Slam Champion in Austin, Texas, finished in the top three her first year competing at Southern Fried. She has been featured in the Texas Observer, For Harriet, Teen Vogue, EASTside Magazine, and The Agenda: working for LGBT economic equality. Ebony has published The Queen's Glory & the Pussy's Box and Love Letters To Balled Fists. Much of her work can be seen on Write About Now Poetry, Button Poetry, and Poetry Slam Inc. YouTube channels. In 2017 Ebony debuted her second one-womxn show, *Ocean*, which won the B. Iden Payne Award for Best Original Script and Outstanding Lead Actress in a Drama. Her first one-womxn show, *Hunger*, in 2015 also won the B. Iden Payne Award for Outstanding Lead Actress in a Drama. She was also nominated for a Payne Award for Outstanding Original Script and won the Austin Critics' Table David Mark Cohen New Play Award. The former Sexual Health Educator with the resting bitch face, sometimes known as The Gully Princess, writes because she has to and eats cupcakes for fun. There's more to this bio, but Ebony hates bios because all that really matters is how she makes you feel.

Ebony Stewart is, #storyoftheblackgirlwinning
http://www.ebpoetry.com/

FORTHCOMING BOOKS BY BUTTON POETRY

Ebony Stewart, *BloodFresh*

Kyle Tran Myhre, *Not a lot of Reasons to Sing, but Enough*

Steven Willis, *A Peculiar People*

Topaz Winters, *So, Stranger*

Siaara Freeman, *Urbanshee*

Junious 'Jay' Ward, *Composition*

Darius Simpson, *Never Catch Me*

Robert Lynn, *How to Maintain Eye Contact*

OTHER BOOKS BY BUTTON POETRY

If you enjoyed this book, please consider checking out some of our others, below. Readers like you allow us to keep broadcasting and publishing. Thank you!

Neil Hilborn, *Our Numbered Days*
Hanif Abdurraqib, *The Crown Ain't Worth Much*
Sabrina Benaim, *Depression & Other Magic Tricks*
Rudy Francisco, *Helium*
Rachel Wiley, *Nothing Is Okay*
Neil Hilborn, *The Future*
Phil Kaye, *Date & Time*
Andrea Gibson, *Lord of the Butterflies*
Blythe Baird, *If My Body Could Speak*
Desireé Dallagiacomo, *SINK*
Dave Harris, *Patricide*
Michael Lee, *The Only Worlds We Know*
Raych Jackson, *Even the Saints Audition*
Brenna Twohy, *Swallowtail*
Porsha Olayiwola, *i shimmer sometimes, too*
Jared Singer, *Forgive Yourself These Tiny Acts of Self-Destruction*
Adam Falkner, *The Willies*
George Abraham, *Birthright*
Omar Holmon, *We Were All Someone Else Yesterday*
Rachel Wiley, *Fat Girl Finishing School*
Bianca Phipps, *crown noble*
Rudy Francisco, *I'll Fly Away*
Natasha T. Miller, *Butcher*
Kevin Kantor, *Please Come Off-Book*
Ollie Schminkey, *Dead Dad Jokes*
Reagan Myers, *Afterwards*
L.E. Bowman, *What I Learned From the Trees*
Patrick Roche, *A Socially Acceptable Breakdown*
Andrea Gibson, *You Better Be Lightning*
Rachel Wiley, *Revenge Body*

Available at buttonpoetry.com/shop and more!